Garden birds

Gardening **organically**

One of the great joys of gardening is to experience the variety of life that a healthy garden contains. A garden managed using organic methods will have far more interest in it than a garden where insecticides and chemicals are used. An organic garden is a more balanced environment, where 'good' creatures such as ladybirds and beetles keep the 'bad' pests and diseases under control. It also provides an excellent environment for birds.

Organically grown plants also tend to be healthier and stronger than plants that rely on large doses of artificial fertiliser. In healthy soil they grow strong roots and can better withstand attack by pests and diseases. Soil can be kept in top condition by recycling garden waste to make nutritious compost. Growing the right combination of plants in the right place at the right time - by rotating where you plant your veg for example, or choosing shrubs to suit the growing conditions that your garden can offer - can deliver impressive disease-free results.

These are the basic principles of organic growing – use the natural resources you already have to create a balanced and vibrant garden. It's sustainable, cheaper than buying chemicals, easier than you think and great fun. Enjoy your organic gardening.

Wild birds bring life to any garden, large or small, with song, colour and movement. And there is now more help on hand than ever before for those of us who love to watch, feed and help them. The UK's gardens are now an important habitat for wild bird conservation; there is lots that we can do to make our gardens even more welcoming to those birds that are losing their countryside habitats. This book shows you which birds you can attract, how to attract more of them and where to find more information.

Contents

Nuthatch

1

Helping birds

Chaffinch

Why help birds?

Gardens play a crucial part in helping birds thrive. Recent research suggests gardens now support important numbers of seriously declining species, such as the song thrush, and that far more birds than previously realised depend on them for a place to nest.

Why are birds declining? Modern industrial farming methods tend to use chemicals to kill pests and weeds – but this destroys a bird's natural food. As a result, over the last fifty years our countryside has, for example, lost 82 per cent of partridges and 75 per cent of skylarks.

In contrast, organic farming and gardening relies on an intact food chain – not pesticides. Organic farms and gardens need predators (such as ladybirds) to feed on pests (such as aphids). This in turn conserves food for the birds. Research shows that more skylark chicks survive on organic farms because their insect food has not been wiped out by pesticides. The government supports organic farming because of its role in conserving wildlife.

You too can help look after wildlife by following organic practices in the garden. Currently, gardens cover large proportions of urban areas, around 23% of Sheffield, for example and 27% of Leicester. By preserving an intact food chain, you will provide life-sustaining food for birds and other wildlife. And it is rewarding when birds make their home in your welcoming garden.

How can we help?

There are two main ways we can all help birds in the garden, providing extra food and water and providing a safe, productive breeding habitat. Most bird lovers feed in winter, when birds certainly need help, but experts now recognise the value of providing extra food all year, to maintain adult birds' condition through the stress of nesting and enable them to spare natural food for their chicks. Also, changing garden management can help birds to breed. As well as safe nest sites, birds need small creatures like caterpillars,

aphids and spiders to feed their chicks. These small animals live on plants but many do not thrive on popular garden plants from other countries. 'Native' plants which originate in this country generally support more wildlife and hence provide more bird food. It is also important to eliminate the use of pesticides which destroy the birds' natural food. Sickness or death through eating poisoned prey is a worry too, particularly for the snail-eating Song Thrush if slug and snail pellets are used. Even 'safe' pesticides need care; and if you use pheromone lures for codling moth, ensure young Blue Tits cannot meet a sticky end inside the trap.

Most garden birds used to live on the edges of forests or in the varied habitat provided by traditional farming. They used different resources at different times of year; tree seed and stubbles for winter food, hedges and scrub for nesting, hundreds of caterpillars for their chicks from native trees and unsprayed fields, plenty of small weed seeds for the fledglings in summer. Different birds nest in different places - some near or even on the ground, others in the treetops; still others in holes. And different birds feed in different ways – on the ground, hanging from twigs, some even in the air; they prefer different kinds of food too and change their diets with the seasons. Blackbirds eat mostly fruit in autumn and winter, mostly worms in spring and summer. Diversity is therefore the keyword if we want to help birds to survive and thrive in our gardens.

Diversity

Diversity is close to the hearts of organic gardeners, who promote a balanced community of pests and their predators that regulates itself without chemicals. Garden birds like Blue Tits eat a wide variety of prey as well as seeds; they depend on a diverse, healthy ecosystem. If they are breeding productively, that suggests their garden home is healthy and in a good ecological balance. Coal miners used Canaries to warn of danger; healthy garden birds show our garden is a healthy space for children, pets and ourselves.

The relationship between birds and organic gardeners is mutually beneficial. Many birds consume garden crops - if allowed - but they also rid the garden of pests. The Song Thrush will eat numerous snails, especially if you provide it with a brick as a shell-smashing 'anvil'. Jays also eat snails, although they may prefer your crops and fruit! Starlings probe the lawn in late summer, searching for root-eating leatherjackets and aerating the grass at the same time. Tits are great caterpillar eaters. A nestbox in an apple tree will reduce the moth and sawfly larvae. Blackbirds forage for cutworms among lettuces, both they and the friendly Robin following your spade snap up wireworms and other soil pests exposed by cultivation. Wrens and Dunnocks remove small insect pests from shrubs and the ground below them.

There are two main ways we can all help birds in the garden, providing extra food and water and providing a safe, productive breeding habitat.

13

action stations

1 **Diversity.** Grow 'native' UK plants to provide the seeds and insects British garden birds like.

2 **Nesting.** Give a range of birds a helping hand by providing nest boxes of varying types and sizes.

3 **Feeding.** Experts recommend that we provide a variety of food for birds all year round.

4 **Pest control.** A healthy population of garden birds will help you to deal with your pest problems – but you may need to protect some of your crops!

5 **Eliminate** the use of pesticides which destroy the birds' natural food.

2

Planning your garden to attract birds

Blackcap – visiting more gardens in winter.

Resources for garden birds

An ideal bird garden will offer several different resources. A feeding station is generally first priority, to help birds through both cold winter weather and the stress of breeding. Nesting sites are easily provided, in boxes, buildings or trees and shrubs.

Cover and nesting sites

Cover is also critical; birds need to hide from predators and even from each other, especially during the annual moult in late summer. The more different types of cover, the more species will visit and even nest in the garden; try especially to provide a range of heights. Finches nest in mature fruit trees,

Song Thrushes in head-high forks, while Blackbirds like hedges. Shrubs conceal Dunnock nests and even the beautifully camouflaged pockets of Long-tailed Tits, especially if the shrub is dense and thorny to deter Magpies. Wrens, Robins and even Blackcaps will nest in waist-high cover such as berberis or cotoneaster (or, better still native, fruit-providing brambles); ground cover plants in rural gardens conceal Willow Warbler nests. A tall mature tree is ideal for Mistle Thrush, Nuthatch and even Tawny Owl, the latter two using nestboxes if provided. Children and pets can disturb nesting birds but if boxes are in quiet corners and youngsters encouraged to take an interest, braver species like Tits and Blackbirds can still do well.

Vegetable enthusiasts can enable Blackbirds and Robins to nest by simply leaving the shed window ajar at all times; many allotments have nestboxes and even hedges, alive with birds. If you prefer decorative borders, sunflowers, cosmos, and teasels allowed to set seed will attract Goldfinches and Greenfinches; the decorative seed pods of honesty even tempt the scarce Bullfinch.

Keeping birds off your veg

Sometimes birds make themselves unwelcome by devouring our hard-won crops. Woodpigeons are unpopular with brassica growers; barriers such as netting are the only effective deterrent although the moving reflections of suspended compact discs can also help.

A well-trained dog is another effective Pigeon (and cat) deterrent!

A fruit cage is the best way to keep birds off soft fruit. If netting is used, set it tidily and check it regularly as birds can become entangled. Threads suspended between sticks at bird height to disrupt the birds' movement are a safer method of protecting seeds and fleece can provide protection from birds as well as weather. In America model owls are a popular bird deterrent and model cats with lifelike glass eyes have also been used. However, birds quickly get used to stationary objects, even traditional scarecrows. Some movement, preferably unpredictable, is a great advantage in any bird-scarer.

Birds need a suitable source of food if they are to survive in your garden. An organic garden is more likely to provide a balanced source of food and cover.

The top twenty winter species

The top twenty winter species recorded by BTO/CJ Garden BirdWatch volunteers, with the average percentage of gardens in which they occur between January and March and estimated numbers of breeding pairs in Britain.

1. Blackbird

97% of gardens

4.4 million pairs

Declined recently but recovering somewhat. Very versatile, found in many habitats although rare in open country, prefers to be near cover. Typically nests against trunk of tree or bush but often in or on sheds, buildings and walls, several broods of 3-5 chicks each year. Feeds mostly on ground, flicking leaves and pulling worms out, in autumn and winter takes fruit and berries. Will take almost any artificial food even peanuts, scraps of bread if hungry, but prefers bird tables or ground to hanging feeders. Welcomes dried fruit, stored apples, cake, Christmas pudding!

2. Blue Tit

96% of gardens

3.3 million pairs

Increasing, possibly helped by garden feeding and nestboxes. Highly arboreal (tree-dwelling), adapted to feed in small branches, hence at home on any hanging feeder, enjoying peanuts but preferring black sunflower seeds if provided, eagerly takes fat in winter. Hole nester, uses nestboxes, 25mm minimum entrance hole, one large brood per year, typically 7-8 chicks in gardens, success linked to availability of small caterpillars for feeding chicks.

3. Robin

92% of gardens

4.2 million pairs

Stable or slightly increasing. Tame gardener's friend in Britain (interestingly, continental birds are shy), mainly eats insects, worms and other small prey but takes fat in winter, cake crumbs, small scraps and even sunflower hearts from some hanging feeders. Cup nest is usually well-hidden in wall cavity, shrubs against wall, ivy, outbuilding, even rubbish heap, generally 2 broods of 4-6 chicks. Noisy chicks are very vulnerable to predators.

4. Chaffinch

83% of gardens

5.4 million pairs

Increased in 70s and 80s but now stable. Quite tame, common around picnic areas, cafes, etc. Associated with traditional farms particularly in north and west. Takes wide range of seeds in winter, generally from the ground, but in breeding season eats mostly insects and small caterpillars. Uses feeders, particularly black sunflower seeds. Small, neat nest in forked branch of large bush or small tree, generally one brood of 3-6 chicks.

5. Dunnock

81% of gardens

2 million pairs   Amber listed

Declined substantially, 'amber-listed' (medium conservation concern). Ground-feeding insect-eater, finds small prey and tiny crumbs among leaf litter and soil, can learn to take sunflower hearts from feeders. Likes small seeds such as nyjer and chicory, will use tables if near cover but prefers ground. Nest in dense hedges and shrubs, waist-high or even lower but hard to spot, two broods of 4-6 chicks. Complex social life, often more than one male per female, favourite host of the cuckoo. Does well in cities and industrial estates, exploiting shrubberies and food crumbs.

6. Great Tit

81% of gardens

1.6 million pairs

Steady and continuing increase since 1960s. Feeds on ground more than smaller tits, particularly on beech nuts, but very quick to adapt to new foods and agile and versatile on feeders although, like all tits, prefers to take seed and eat in cover. Hole nester, 28mm minimum nestbox entrance, different tit species nest quite close together so provide more than one box if both Blues and Greats are around. Breeding success linked to supply of natural food for chicks, one brood per year, typically 5-8 chicks in gardens, will sometimes breed twice if first brood fails.

7. Collared Dove

76% of gardens
200,000 pairs

Colonised Britain in 1955, rapid increase ever since. Small non-native dove associated with human habitations, relatively uncommon in rural areas. May depend to some extent on artificial food, takes all kinds of seed and grain from tables and ground, can perch on larger feeders, especially if a tray is fitted. Flimsy stick platform nest in almost any tree or shrub. Only lays two eggs at a time but breeds repeatedly in almost any month, given food and mild temperatures.

8. Greenfinch

76% of gardens
530,000 pairs

Increasing since 1990s, possibly helped by climate change. Seed eater, large powerful bill tackles tough fruits, rose hips, shells and seeds without using feet, particularly fond of black sunflower seeds. Feeds from all kinds of feeders, tables and ground, quite aggressive and dominant but very prone to salmonella infections, care with hygiene needed. Most nest in the countryside, visiting gardens for food, but will use dense rural garden hedges and bushes; often nests in loose colonies producing two or three broods of 3-6 chicks.

9. House Sparrow

77% of gardens

3.6 million pairs ● Red listed

Severe decline over last 25 years, 'red-listed' (serious conservation concern). A 'commensal' species i.e. now depends on human activities for food and nest sites. Needs reliable supply of seed or grain close to bushes or hedges in which noisy flocks can socialise. Readily uses feeders and tables, will eat grain if good quality seeds not available. Can be a nuisance in numbers but large flocks are now rare. Nests in cavities in buildings or nest boxes with 32mm minimum entrance, placed a few feet apart under the eaves near an existing colony. Three or even four broods of 3-6 chicks, nesting performance depends on availability of small insects to feed the chicks, an increasing problem as urban habitats are 'cleaned up'.

10. Woodpigeon

56% of gardens

2.4 million pairs

Rapid increase since 1970s helped by agricultural change and warmer winters, ever more on bird tables and in urban areas. Large and hungry, devours alarming quantities of food from tables and ground, storing seeds or peanuts in large crop before retiring to cover to digest in safety. Strips green vegetable crops bare if allowed, surprisingly agile for such a large bird, will even use some seed feeders and briefly hang upside down. Fond of ivy berries. Flimsy stick platform nest in almost any medium-height tree or bush, including street trees, only two eggs but several broods per year.

11. Starling

74% of gardens

1.1 million pairs   ● Red listed

Severe decline, 'red-listed' (serious conservation concern). Large numbers used to feed on traditional meadows in summer, now more dependent on lawns and artificial food. Agile and quick to learn, adapts to any hanging food, very fond of fat in winter. Natural foods are soil-dwellers such as worms and leatherjackets but takes more or less anything edible from crusts to meat scraps. Generally relies on building cavities to nest, uses large nest boxes with 45mm entrance, normally only one brood of 4-7 chicks.

12. Magpie

52% of gardens

600,000 pairs

Large recent increase has stabilised although still moving into some urban areas. Comfortable among human habitations but still often wary. Large, omnivorous refuse operative cleans up urban unpleasantness from dog droppings to takeaways, relishes meat scraps, takes seed from tables especially if high quality like sunflower hearts, notoriously takes eggs and chicks from nests of other birds. Builds unmistakeable large domed nest in almost any street tree or large bush. Territorial nesting pairs produce one brood of 5-8 chicks, many others live in loose 'singles' flocks.

13. Coal Tit

48% of gardens

600,000 pairs

Rapid increase to mid-70s, likes conifers so responded well to maturing post-war pine plantations. Loves black sunflower seeds, but unlike Blue and Great Tits is a hoarder, removing numerous seeds from feeders and storing them for hard times. Will use nest boxes with 25mm minimum entrance, often nests near ground, sometimes even in abandoned mouse holes, one brood of 6-9 chicks. Agile and thin-billed, natural food is tiny insects among pine needles and cones, adapts to any hanging feeder although sometimes bullied by larger species.

14. Wren

43% of gardens

7.1 million pairs

Increased in mid-70s but numbers fluctuate, this tiny bird is sensitive to cold winters but still one of our most abundant species. Probably nests in many more gardens than the 43% used for winter feeding. Mainly insect eater tempted by crumbs or small seeds such as nyjer in hard weather and will try fat or even peanuts if desperate. Males build several domed nests well-hidden in dense bushes, boxes, wall cavities or sheds, of which the female chooses her favourite. Normally two broods of 5-8 chicks.

15. Goldfinch

21% of gardens

220,000 pairs

Declined sharply to mid-80s but since recovered, many more visiting gardens and urban areas recently. Easily attracted with teasels (especially if the heads are refilled with nyjer seed) but rapidly graduate to black sunflower seeds. Sociable birds, especially in winter, tiny neat nest in the branches of a bush or hedge, even in surprisingly busy spots such as supermarket car parks or industrial estates. Two, sometimes three broods of 4-6 chicks.

16. Song Thrush

35% of gardens

990,000 pairs   Red listed

Severe decline since mid-70s but slightly stabilising now, 'red-listed' (serious conservation concern). Remaining birds are strongly associated with gardens, using lawns for feeding, large bushes or small trees for nesting (normally in a fork at head height) and shrubs for protection. Open, mud-lined nests are vulnerable to predators, but ability to produce three broods of 3-5 chicks compensates in good habitat. Readily takes bird table supplies in winter, particularly scraps, fat, cake and dried fruit.

15

16

17

18

17. Long-tailed Tit

27% of gardens
210,000 pairs

Fluctuating with winter weather, no clear trend but adapting to urban areas and artificial foods, particularly peanuts and fat in winter. Extremely light and agile, hunts tiny insects among the thinnest twigs, gleans for spiders and moths around window frames. Highly sociable in winter, feeding and roosting together in small flocks. Remarkable pocket nest of moss, lichen, spiders' webs and (in urban areas) styrofoam, well-camouflaged in a thorny bush or brambles. One brood of 7-12 chicks but vulnerable to predation; birds whose nests are destroyed often help to rear the chicks of a relative instead of re-building.

18. Carrion Crow

27% of gardens
970,000 pairs

Steady, continuing increase since 1960s, increasing colonisation of urban areas exploiting edible refuse and garden food. Powerful nest predators, even destroying eggs and chicks of Magpies, these large, noisy birds are full of character and interest but less than welcome in many smaller gardens. Numbers probably limited by need for tall, mature trees for their very large open nests although as more post-war street trees mature, more sites become available. One brood of 4-6 chicks. Replaced in northern Scotland by the grey and black Hooded Crow.

19. Jackdaw

22% of gardens

390,000 pairs

Moderate continuing increase since 1960s, has appeared in some urban areas although these quite conservative, highly sociable birds seem at home in some towns but not others. Generally more common in north and west. Our smallest crow, very agile but relatively shy, sneaks onto bird tables and hanging feeders early in the morning when we are asleep, takes refuse and scraps like other crows. Prefers to breed in a loose colony, often using chimneys, also cavities in old walls and even nestboxes with 150mm minimum entrance hole.

20. Great Spotted Woodpecker

20% of gardens

28,000 pairs

Rapid increase in 70s and 90s. Did well out of dutch elm disease and is surprisingly common in gardens in winter, so may be benefiting from artificial food. Takes peanuts all winter and brings entertaining youngsters to learn how to use feeders in June. Versatile feeder, eats seeds, nuts and insects extracted from dead trees; sometimes also smashes nestboxes to remove young birds and destroys House Martin nests. Normally excavates nest hole in dead tree but will use a large nestbox (50mm entrance hole) if it is filled with styrofoam or sawdust for the birds to remove.

19

20

*Berries and windfall apples
will help Blackbirds and
Thrushes through the winter,
including winter migrants
such as Fieldfare (left) and
Redwing.*

Scarcer garden visitors that
need our help:

- **Bullfinch**. 'Red-listed', this beautiful bird has lost much of its rural habitat and will now nest even in urban gardens and take black sunflower seeds if the feeder is close to cover and undisturbed.

- **Reed Bunting**. 'Red-listed', this was a characteristic bird of winter farmland but is now being helped by sunflower hearts in an increasing number of gardens.

- **Tree Sparrow**. 'Red-listed', the smaller, neater cousin of the House Sparrow likes peanuts and seeds and will use nestboxes, but is normally only found in rural gardens.

- **Mistle Thrush**. 'Amber-listed', this large and beautiful thrush needs a tall tree to nest in but is surprisingly common in some urban areas.

  Tawny Owl. Little is known about owl numbers but they are worryingly scarce, nonetheless this large, spectacular nocturnal predator will nest and hunt even in urban gardens, especially if a special nestbox is provided.

Top from left, Bullfinch and Tree Sparrow.
Second row from left, Tawny Owl,
Mistle Thrush, and Reed Bunting.
Scarcer garden birds can be helped if
you pay particular attention to habitat,
nesting and feeding requirements.

Ten ways of increasing the number of birds in your garden.

- Provide a range of different foods

- Provide a selection of different types of habitat and cover

- Provide water

- Try to find space for a medium-sized native tree

- Try to safeguard the birds from predators – a dog is the best cat repellent!

- Don't be over-tidy

- Ban use of herbicides and pesticides

- Discourage cats

- Don't plant non-native plants

- Don't disturb nests

3

Feeding

Natural **food** and extra food

Gardens offer birds several different kinds of food. Firstly, we must not forget the natural food provided by the garden's own ecosystem, with help from its owner. Invertebrates (insects, spiders, worms, snails, etc.) are vital for baby birds; native plants, habitat diversity and minimising pesticides will help them. However, a bird garden can also provide natural winter food: fruit and berries (ideally of native species), apples, brambles, holly, ivy and yew. Water is also vital, both in winter and summer, for plumage maintenance as well as drinking.

Dry feed

Dry foods, mainly seeds and peanuts, are the most convenient supplementary bird foods. Peanut kernels either in 'red bags' or modern mesh feeders will be enjoyed by young Sparrows, Long-tailed Tits and

If your budget runs to it you can even provide live food such as mealworms.

Great Spotted Woodpeckers even when other foods are provided. In the breeding season, ensure only small fragments can be removed to prevent whole nuts choking chicks. Old-fashioned 'monkey nuts' are usually ignored if better food is available nearby. An excellent food for most small garden birds is black sunflower seeds, which are grown for oil extraction and so have thin skins and high fat content as well as being protein-rich. They will help a much wider range of species (and the garden will be tidier) if bought ready-husked, the so-called 'sunflower hearts'. Other pure seeds available include wheat grain, which is only really suitable for Pigeons, Ducks and hungry Sparrows, nyjer, a tiny seed enjoyed by Dunnocks and Goldfinches and oatmeal which is nutritious but spoils in the rain. In rural areas, sacks of oilseed rape or linseed bought from farms are a cheap way of feeding winter Finch flocks in larger gardens.

Mix, blend or single seed?

Many gardeners prefer to buy seed mixes, assuming that a blend will benefit more birds. In fact, this is rarely the case except with more expensive softbill mixes or fruit-rich 'high-energy' blends from specialist suppliers. Most economical seed mixes contain some foods birds like, such as black sunflower seeds or hearts, and some that are less popular, such as wheat. Most birds simply sift out the goodies and discard the rest. So purchasing specific seeds such as sunflower hearts or nyjer may be more efficient.

Organic seed

Considering the poor choice of food available to birds in winter, especially in urban areas, and the short natural life spans of most wild birds (typically less than one year) paying extra for organic seeds may appear a luxury, but in fact supporting organic growers promotes a more bird- and wildlife-friendly countryside as well.

Live food

In the breeding season, those of us who can afford to, buy live foods such as earthworms, mealworm or waxworms. This will make life much easier for hard-working parent birds, especially in urban habitats. Mealworms are beetle larvae, a common natural food; although their tough jaws could damage very young chicks, so parent birds usually stun them against a branch before presenting them to their babies. Waxworms are moth larvae and hence even closer to the birds' ideal natural food; sadly they too are usually quite expensive.

Fat cakes

Fat cakes and balls are increasingly popular and very successful in helping birds through the winter. They can be hung or simply stood on tables – ideally secured so larger birds such as Magpies do not remove them whole. Best of all are the fat bars mixed with peanut flour and other high-protein ingredients, which may even include dried insects. A simple home-made alternative is unsalted lard

Yellowhammer

melted and mixed with blended porridge oats, allowed to set in a biscuit or drink can. This soft mixture does not keep well in warm weather but is an economical way to help Starlings and Tits in winter.

Many household scraps can be fed to birds although again this is best restricted to winter when birds need high-calorie supplements and leftovers are less likely to spoil or attract rats. Starlings love a chicken carcase and even with top quality foods available, it is amazing how many Sparrows will still avidly snatch a crust of white bread. Stored fruit such as apple is ideal for Thrushes and if your budget can stretch to dried fruit like sultanas, you will be very popular and may even be able to hand-tame the Blackbirds. It is kinder to soak dried fruit before presenting it if it is old and hard.

Storing food

Bird food should be stored in dry and cool conditions; it quickly spoils if damp and warm. Spoiled seed at best loses nutritional value and at worst can poison birds. A cool garage or cellar is ideal, wooden sheds often get rather hot. To deter mice and rats, bird food is best kept in strong metal bins, these can be bought specially but an old-fashioned galvanised dustbin made redundant by wheelie-bins is perfect.

Selecting a feeder

Returning to the theme of diversity, different birds like to feed in different ways and places. Some, like Blackbirds and Dunnocks, are ground-feeders, others, like Tits, feed hanging from branches. Try to provide feeding stations of different kinds and at different heights.

Siskin

Different birds like to feed in different ways. Try to provide feeding stations of different kinds and at different heights.

Wren

Acrobatic species like Starlings, Sparrows and Nuthatch do not need perches to feed from, they can cling to any feeder at any angle. Finches generally prefer to perch. Modern feeders have 'ports', each of which accommodates a single bird, the latest designs have perching rings on which the birds can comfortably face their food rather than awkwardly feeding sideways.

The grey squirrel, an alien species introduced from North America, can be a serious problem at feeders, consuming huge quantities of food and deterring birds. 'Squirrel-proof' feeders like the 'Nuttery' range surround the food with a tough wire cage through which small birds can enter, other spring-loaded or even motorised anti-squirrel devices are available. Many ingenious 'home-brew' squirrel deterrents have been devised such as mounting feeders on smooth metal poles with floppy plastic 'baffles' and hanging feeders from long thin steel cables, with spinning plastic bottles. An alternative approach is to provide separate food specifically for the squirrels but remember the grey squirrel is a nest predator which, unlike the birds, is doing pretty well without our help.

The '**menu**' at an **ideal bird garden** might read as follows:

- Large multi-port seed feeder for Finches and Sparrows, ideally sunflower hearts but seed mix if cost is a consideration.

- Small black sunflower seed or heart feeder for the Tits.

- Small peanut feeder for Long-tailed Tits and Woodpeckers.

- Fat balls or bars for Starlings and Robins – some hanging, some accessible from branches or bird table.

- Bird table with seed and scraps for Thrushes and Blackbirds, Doves and other larger species.

- Fruit and scraps on the ground, some near cover for the shyer birds like Wrens and Dunnocks, some in the open to distract the Woodpigeons.

- And of course, water.

Hygiene

Birds can transmit serious infections to each other at busy feeding stations, not only when the weather is warm and bacteria breed rapidly but also when birds are in poor condition in winter. Salmonella is a particular problem and this can also infect pets and even children or the elderly. Hence, all bird feeders should be kept reasonably clean and basic hygiene precautions such as hand washing should always be observed. Usually clean water and a stiff brush is all that's needed to remove droppings but a splash of cheap unperfumed bleach in a bucket of water can help ensure safety – especially if sickly or dead birds have been found. Rinse feeders with clean water afterwards and let them dry before refilling. Sick birds are hungry and they will come to where food is abundant but this does not mean you have infected them. If you do see sick birds, it's vital to keep your feeders clean to prevent subsequent transmission of their illness to other healthy birds.

All bird feeders should be kept reasonably clean and basic hygiene precautions such as hand washing should always be observed.

Drinking and bathing

Water is as vital in winter for plumage maintenance as it is in summer for drinking. Bird baths and water dishes quickly become fouled and need regular cleaning, remember to break the ice in winter, float a small plastic ball to reduce freezing or fill them afresh from the kettle each morning. Never add salt or other chemicals, salt is toxic to garden birds. If a garden pond is designed sensibly with a shallow area at the edge to allow birds to drink and bathe this will attract more species than a simple dish, especially if it is near cover, and may even provide tadpoles for the Blackbirds.

House Sparrows

Season-by-season bird feeding tips

Winter (December – February)

In the coldest weather birds need maximum energy in the minimum time; days are short and competition at feeders can be fierce, especially when winter visitors from northern Europe join our resident birds. Provide high calorie foods like fat balls and bars, fatty meat, cake and pudding scraps as well as peanuts and black sunflower seeds or hearts. Remember birds need water too, even in freezing weather, to maintain their plumage. Stored fruit such as apples will help Thrushes in late winter, perhaps even attracting Fieldfare and Redwing.

Spring (March – May)

Late winter visitors like Brambling and Siskin will eat large amounts of black sunflower seed but resident birds start to nest and incubate their eggs, so will be less conspicuous. Specialist suppliers add crushed shell ('oystershell grit') to food mixes to help female birds build their eggshells. Reduce the high-fat foods unless the weather turns cold and be sure to match supply to demand – food allowed to accumulate and spoil is very bad for birds. Minimise the time females need to leave their eggs by providing high-quality, efficient foods like sunflower hearts. When eggs hatch, activity will increase; consider providing live food for the chicks and ensure only small fragments of peanuts can be taken from proper mesh feeders.

Summer (June-August)

Many young fledglings will seek food and shelter from predators in our gardens. Peanuts are popular with young Sparrows and Woodpeckers, soft, small peanut granules are also good. High-energy fruit-rich mixtures presented near cover will help young Blackbirds and Thrushes. Family parties of young Tits and Finches will appreciate black sunflower seed or hearts. Consider using ultrasonic cat deterrents to protect young birds at feeding stations. Ensure water is available and do not let food spoil in hot weather.

Autumn (September – November)

Finches and Thrushes may still have fledglings to feed but by October most garden feeders go quiet as birds depart to exploit abundant food in the countryside. However those that remain are moulting and hence under stress, they will benefit greatly from high-protein food like sunflower hearts and even live food but be sure to match supply to demand. If food is scarce in the countryside, young Starlings and Finches will show up in late autumn expecting you to start providing their winter menu.

action stations

1 **Hygiene.** Keep feeders and water sources clean and fresh.

2 **Seasons.** Learn about what birds need at different times of the year but don't put out too much food and let it spoil.

3 **Feeders.** There is a very wide range of different types of feeder – select the ones that suit the birds you want to attract.

Mistle Thrush

4

Providing a home

Who nests where?

Trees and large bushes: Thrushes, Finches, Pigeons and Doves, Crows and Magpies

Small bushes, shrubs and tall borders: Dunnock, Long-tailed Tit, Chiffchaff, Blackcap

Houses and other large buildings: House Sparrow, Starling, Swift, House Martin, Tits

Sheds and outbuildings: Robin, Blackbird, Wren, Swallow

Walls and creepers: Robin, Pied Wagtail, Wren, Blackbird, Spotted Flycatcher, Tits if wall cavities available

Chimneys: Jackdaw, Stock Dove

Standard nestboxes: Tits (*Blue Tit opposite, top left*) and Sparrows, Nuthatch, Wren, Pied Flycatcher (in north and west), Redstart

Open-front nestboxes: Robin, Wren, Pied Wagtail

Special nestboxes: Starling, Great Spotted Woodpecker, House Martin, Swallow, *(opposite, top right),* Swift, Spotted Flycatcher, Treecreeper, Tawny Owl, Jackdaw, Kestrel *(opposite, bottom right),* Stock Dove.

Treecreeper

Siting a nestbox

Many people worry about the best place to site a nestbox - in fact any nestbox in any place is better than no box at all and birds often choose surprising sites. The golden rules are to avoid facing the box into a cold prevailing wind and to try to prevent driving rain from entering the hole; slope the box slightly downwards at the front rather than tilting it backwards. Boxes should also not be sited where strong afternoon sun will bake the chicks. Birds use temperature regulation as an important cue in choosing a hole; a thick box that provides good insulation may be successful in an unpromising site, whereas a thin, damp plywood box may fail to attract a tenant even in the best possible position. Providing a choice of boxes greatly increases the chances of success. Birds of the same species maintain a certain distance between their nests but birds of different species can nest close together.

Top tips for a successful nestbox

Good nestboxes are available from specialist suppliers, those made from 'woodcrete' are particularly durable and successful. Alternatively, boxes are easy to make and birds use a wide range of shapes and sizes. 32mm is the best general purpose hole diameter and good thick wood is more important than skilled carpentry. Ensure the lid is watertight and overhangs the entrance, drill small drainage holes in the base and hinge the lid with tyre inner tube if you wish to inspect the box or clean it out in late September, as most experts recommend. It is best not to disturb boxes in winter as they may be in use by roosting birds. Never fit a perch; hole-nesting birds do not need one, only predators benefit. Check nestboxes annually and repair any damage, particularly warping, splitting or perished hinges that might allow water in to chill the chicks. If squirrels damage the entrance holes, fit metal plates.

Watching birds

Cheap over-powered or zoom binoculars can be very hard to use, a standard size like 8 x 40 is more practical and simply buy the best you can afford. Mail order suppliers advertise in birdwatching magazines or on the Internet. Check minimum focus distance though, some cheap binoculars may not be able to focus on your bird table from your favourite chair. Most binoculars will focus through modern 'float' glass but older window glass may blur your view. It is surprisingly easy to obtain good photographs of feeding birds with cheap equipment; a lens of 200mm focal length or even less will enable close-up shots of birds on a table by your window; poke the lens between closed curtains to minimise disturbance. Digital cameras open up even more possibilities, especially if used with a telescope ('digiscoping'); if you want more information on this, there are many enthusiasts' web sites with more information.

House Sparrows can be given a helping hand with the installation of a community nesting box on a quiet sheltered wall.

Predators

It is very important to try not to feed birds in any way that makes them more vulnerable to predators. **Cats and Sparrowhawks** may learn to associate busy feeders with easy prey; if this is a problem try siting your feeders close to cover or perhaps even placing them right inside a hedge or bush. Cut back bushes at the base to prevent cats from hiding and consider ultrasonic deterrents such as 'Catwatch'; although expensive these are effective and they work even better if moved slightly every 10 days or so to keep the cats guessing. Sadly, a few cats are deaf!

Magpies too rob nests to feed their own young which can be distressing; luckily the Magpie only has one single brood of chicks per year so earlier and later broods of their prey species often survive. Boost the survival chances of young birds by providing dense and preferably thorny bushes and hedges for nesting; never prune a hedge in the nesting season if Magpies are around, they will quickly notice disturbed nesting birds and harry them persistently if their location is carelessly revealed. It may be necessary to actually surround threatened nests with a cage or panels of wire mesh, if this is done after the chicks have hatched the parent birds are unlikely to desert them.

Finding **information** and providing it...

The **British Trust for Ornithology** (BTO) publishes a nest box guide with construction details for a wide range of species, see their web site or write (see below) for details. For a free, comprehensive bird feeding and care catalogue contact **CJ Wildbird Foods**, The Rea, Upton Magna, SY4 4UR, tel 0800 731 2820 or see www.birdfood.co.uk.

Both the BTO and RSPB collect information about garden birds from volunteers to help their bird conservation research – and you can help too. The BTO/CJ Garden BirdWatch runs year-round and can be joined at any time; a small annual subscription covers running costs and entitles participants to a garden bird book and a quarterly magazine.

All you need to do is keep us informed about the birds you see in your garden. Contact GBW, **BTO**, the Nunnery, Thetford, IP24 2PU, tel 01842 750050 or see www.bto.org for details. The RSPB Big Garden BirdWatch runs for one day every year in January, contact BGBW, **RSPB**, The Lodge, Sandy, Bedfordshire SG19 2DL or see www.rspb.org.uk.

CJ WildBird Foods Ltd

The Garden Wildlife Specialists

The UK's garden wildlife is facing a brighter future thanks to the work of CJ WildBird Foods. This award-winning company offers quality foods, feeders and nest boxes for birds and other wildlife. Their mail-order delivery service is fast, reasonably priced and operates throughout the UK. CJ's products are also stocked in retail outlets nationwide including Sainsburys and Tescos.

CJ's success has been achieved through education and advice, developing innovative new products and by providing the highest levels of service to their customers.

To find out more or to request a FREE Handbook of Garden Wildlife call freephone **0800 731 2820** or visit **www.birdfood.co.uk**

CJ WildBird Foods kindly supplied the photography for this book. To view more wildlife images or buy online, visit **www.thewildlifelibrary.com**

Want more organic gardening help?

Then join HDRA, the national charity for organic gardening, farming and food.

As a member of HDRA you'll gain-
- free access to our Gardening Advisory Service
- access to our three gardens in Warwickshire, Kent and Essex and to 10 more gardens around the UK
- opportunities to attend courses and talks or visit other gardens on Organic Gardens Open Weekends
- discounts when ordering from the Organic Gardening Catalogue
- discounted membership of the Heritage Seed Library
- quarterly magazines full of useful information

You'll also be supporting-
- the conservation of heritage seeds
- an overseas organic advisory service to help small-scale farmers in the tropics
- Duchy Originals HDRA Organic Gardens for Schools
- HDRA Organic Food For All campaign
- research into organic agriculture

To join HDRA ring: 024 7630 3517
email: enquiries@hdra.org.uk
or visit our website: www.hdra.org.uk

Charity No. 298104

HDRA
the organic organisation

Resources

HDRA the organic organisation promoting organic gardening farming and food
www.hdra.org.uk
024 7630 3517

Soil Association the heart of organic food and farming
www.soilassociation.org
0117 929 0661

BTO
– the British Trust for Ornithology
www.bto.org

RSPB – the Royal Society for the Protection of Birds
www.rspb.org.uk

Organic UK Advice and support for organic gardeners
www.organicgarden.org.uk

MAIL ORDER:

The Organic Gardening Catalogue
Organic seeds, composts, raised beds, barriers, traps and other organic gardening sundries. All purchases help to fund the HDRA's charity work.
www.organiccatalogue.com
0845 1301304

Burns Pet Nutrition Ltd
– organic bird food
www.realfoodforbirds.co.uk
01554 890482

CJ Wildbird Foods Ltd
www.birdfood.co.uk
0800 731 2820

Green Gardener – live bird food
www.greengardener.co.uk
01394 420087

Wiggly Wigglers
– dried and live mealworms
www.wigglywigglers.co.uk
0800 216990

who, what, where, when and why organic?

for all the answers and tempting offers go to www.whyorganic.org

- Mouthwatering offers on organic produce
- Organic places to shop and stay across the UK
- Seasonal recipes from celebrity chefs
- Expert advice on your food and health
- Soil Association food club – join for just £1 a month

Soil Association
the heart of organic food & farming